Cont

Foreword to the Revised Ed.	
Foreword to the First Edition	iii
Introduction	v
Orientation	ix
Part One - Two Views	**1**
The Popular View	3
A Biblical Alternative	7
Part Two - Understanding Hermeneutics	**13**
The Dangers of Literalism: Turning Bread into Stones	15
Isolating the Presuppositions	17
Part Three - Relevant Passages	**21**
Discovering Daniel's Diamond	23
The Olivet Discourse	31
Reveling In Revelation	35
Part Four - Terms and Concepts	**41**
"Ages"	43
Everything You Wanted to Know about the Antichrist	45
Kingdom of God or Kingdom of Heaven?	51
The Secret Rapture	53
The Times of the Gentiles	55
Of Israel and Jews	57
Part Five - The Conclusion of the Matter	**63**
What Difference Does It Make?	65
A Cloud of Witnesses	69
How Then Shall We Live?	71
Where Do We Go from Here?	73
Notes	**75**

ONE DAY

A BIBLICAL ALTERNATIVE TO THE POPULAR VIEW OF THE END TIMES

Daniel E. Collver

Copyright ©1990, 2011 Daniel E. Collver

Revised edition, April 2011

All Rights Reserved

ISBN: 1461046890
ISBN-13: 978-1461046899

Scripture quotations are from THE HOLY BIBLE, NEW INTERNATIONAL VERSION®, NIV® Copyright © 1973, 1978, 1984, 2011 by Biblica, Inc.™ Used by permission. All rights reserved worldwide.

This booklet is dedicated to my dad,

who was always there when I needed him,

and who now lives with the Lord Jesus Christ.

"Lord, where we are wrong, make us willing to change;

where we are right, make us easy to live with."

— *Peter Marshall*

Foreword to the Revised Edition

I originally wrote *One Day* about twenty years ago. While much has transpired both in my life and in our world, little has changed with regards to my prophetical understanding. I have come to realize that my understanding of Scripture is by and large what we would call Reformed theology. I did not set out to become Reformed (at least not in the sense used here), but am gratified to find myself in agreement with so many great men of God.

I confess that I find myself feeling a little like the child in the story of *The Emperor's New Clothes*! Just as he declared that the king "has nothing on" I can't see a thread of evidence for the popular view of end times. I don't know how many of my fellow believers are merely parroting the descriptions of rascal weavers so that they will not be regarded as unfit for office or exceptionally dull, but I for one, am not afraid to cry out "Clothe yourself—you should be ashamed walking around with nothing to hide your shame!" I feel much like the minister who was first sent in to see the work underway on the king's new garments. He thought to himself, *Heaven save us! Is it possible that I am a fool! I have never thought it, and nobody must know it. Is it true that I am unfit for my office? It will never do for me to say that I cannot see the stuff.* Like him, I cannot see "the stuff." Unlike him, I will clearly say I cannot see "the stuff"! If this little booklet causes you to reevaluate your position, to pose questions to authority figures or modify your thinking even an iota, then it will have accomplished its purpose.

One Day

I want to express a very special thanks to my personal editor, Irene, you are a blessing indeed! Thank you also to Dutch Mostert for the use of his painting titled Sunrise Bridge as a cover (*http://raftisland.com/dutch*). Thanks to Don Sanne for illustrating the popular view. Last, but not least, thanks to my son Aaron for spending so much time making this document appear presentable!

Foreword to the First Edition

Do you find the differing views of the end times confusing and difficult to grasp? If so, then you should appreciate the perspective offered here. It is biblical, simple, and easy to understand. While not ignoring the fact that difficulties arise with each differing view, the *One Day* view offers something the other views often seem to miss: it takes the *clear* Scriptures as the guide and lets the difficult ones fall into place if they will, as opposed to allowing obscure passages to distort the clear meaning of the Bible. I hope you will enjoy this booklet and that it will help you in your personal pilgrimage.

I would like to take this space to offer a special note of thanks to those helped at various stages of this booklet: Tom, Peggy, Greg R., Greg C., Garry, and my loving wife, Beth.

Introduction

Sometimes it is helpful to know "where a writer is coming from." What is the author's background? Why is he writing? I am compelled here to reveal a little of my background, which I feel entitles me to share my persuasions in booklet form.

As a young person I grew up in a Southern Baptist church. I had no idea that anyone knew any more about Christ's return other than the fact that one day He would return! When I was old enough to leave home, I rejected God's plan for my life and set out upon a course of worldly living. Eventually, I became convinced of God's existence and of His involvement in my life. Even as a hippie living in a commune and hitchhiking around the country, I read the Bible and prayed. Though I didn't have a great deal of understanding, I did acknowledge the truth and tried to live by it to the degree that I understood it. As I became involved in different eastern religions and cults, I left them as soon as I understood where they departed from the clear truth of the Bible.

Gradually the Lord led me away from a counter-cultural lifestyle and back into a productive way of living. I began attending a Christian fellowship group at the local college and joined a small community church. I also became involved in an enthusiastic Bible study on a regular basis. It was at one of these studies that a pastor, whom I greatly love and respect, taught us about the *pretribulational/premillennial* return of Christ. As a young Christian I was greatly impressed. I ignorantly assumed that what he had just taught me was "gospel truth" and that now I could tell others this same truth!

One Day

That very evening I dropped by my folks' home to share this profound "truth" with them. What *I* didn't know was that there were other views on the matter! They did know. My newfound zeal was somewhat suppressed at that point. All the same, I trusted the man who taught me this view, whether or not I could understand all of the details and ramifications of that viewpoint.

Shortly after this experience I attended a Bible college in the Pacific Northwest. Prior to classes several of us students would sit around and discuss theology, and on occasion we would refer to our end time positions. Those of us who were "really spiritual" opted for a "post-tribulational" view. After three years of intense Bible instruction and reflection I left Bible school with a very clear position on the end times. It was an "I don't know position." By then I was thoroughly confused regarding the Lord's return. I was a "pan-man," that is, whatever pans out!

Since graduating from Bible College I have read and reread the Bible a number of times, noting in particular what it says regarding the end times. I have spent countless hours making note cards, laying out diagrams, spreading out three-by-five cards all over the floor, and trying to make sense out of all that I've discovered. I have often been frustrated and contemplated going back to my "pan" position. And yet, each time I gained something, some insight, some measure of understanding that propelled me to the next level. Having served as both pastor and teacher, I felt a need to comprehend more of what the Scripture taught before I could teach others. As a result, I was driven to a position that ultimately led to my resignation of a pastorate. I have come to hold a position that

Introduction

I refer to as the "One Day" position. That is the position I will present in the following pages. I believe the Bible most clearly teaches that the Return of Christ, the Resurrection, the Rapture, and the Judgment will all take place in *"one day."*

I am not attempting to create an authoritative work; rather, I desire to express an educated opinion about what I believe the Bible teaches. Many of the thoughts here were pointed out and clarified to me by others, so I cannot take a great deal of credit for "original" thinking. It would be wonderful to know the original languages of the Bible, but it is not necessary in order to hold decided positions. This is readily demonstrated by those who are fluent in the original languages yet are poles apart in their theology! I believe that Scripture can speak clearly to us in our native tongue if we allow it to do so. Where I have felt the need, I have both looked up and listened to those who define the Greek and Hebrew words for us. The real question, however, is not whether we know the original languages, but whether we listen to the language we know!

Orientation

In discussions with both pastors and laypeople, I find that a "fog" surrounds the subject of eschatology, the study of last things. To make things as clear as possible from the beginning, let's define a few basic terms that we will use in this booklet.

The Rapture

The *rapture* is a name given to that event which is to occur when the Lord Jesus returns to resurrect the dead saints and deliver the living believers from what takes place on the earth.

The Tribulation

The *tribulation* is thought by many to be a seven-year period (usually in the future), where those who dwell on the earth will undergo great troubles. There are basically four or five views presented as follows:

- Pre-tribulationalism: This view believes that a rapture will occur prior to the tribulation period.

- Mid-tribulationalism: Those who hold this view believe that the Lord will rapture the saints about halfway through the tribulation period.

- Post-tribulationalism: This view teaches that the Lord will not return until after the tribulation has taken place.

- Past-tribulationalism: This view could possibly be referred to as an "atribulational view." This perspective teaches that the tribulation spoken of has been adequately fulfilled historically.

- Pan-tribulationalism: This is the position taken by many who do not have the time, resources, or interest to research and form their own conclusions. They prefer to say, "It will all pan out in the end!"

The tribulation period is generally, if not always, regarded as a separate period prior to a thousand year reign of Christ.

The Millennium

The thousand year reign of Christ is referred to as the *millennium*. There are four popular millennial views.

- Pre-millennialism: This view teaches that Christ will return one thousand years prior to the end of time as we know it and set up an earthly kingdom. During this period Satan will be bound and relative peace will reign on earth. At the very end Satan will be released, gain a following, and ultimately be conquered once and for all by Christ.

- Post-millennialism: This position teaches that conditions on the earth will gradually improve and become more and more "Christianized" until at the end of a millennium Christ will return.

- A-millennialism: This view does not see the Bible as teaching a *literal* thousand year reign of Christ as is commonly taught. This is an unfortunate term since technically the prefix "a" would indicate "without" and literally mean "no millennium." This group believes in a biblical millennium, but not in the same way as it is understood by the other views.

- Pan-millennialism: Similar to the pan-tribulational view.

Orientation

The primary aim at this point is clarify the difference between the terms regarding the tribulation period and the millennium.

Part One

Two Views

The first to present his case seems right, till another comes forward and questions him.

Proverbs 18:17

Chapter One

The Popular View

By and large the most popular view of prophetic events today is the pretribulational/premillennial position (with perhaps the exception of the pantrib/panmil position). While there are probably millions of Christians who do not adhere to the popular view they do not use the available media effectively in order to present their view(s). I sincerely believe that the primary reason for the popularity of the pretrib/premil view is the effective use of mass media. In the past century many television and radio preachers have presented this view as fact so repeatedly that it is often received without question.

It is interesting to note that most of the nuances of this doctrine have only been developed within the past century. Nevertheless, the man or woman who dares to scrutinize the popular view will not rise far in certain evangelical ranks if his or her conclusions dare go "against the grain." Such are the politics of religion. At this point our concern is to understand the basic elements of the popular view. We will not go into the endless details as there is plenty of information readily available to the sincere student. The popular view most simply presented follows these lines:

1. The next great event is the rapture.
2. After the rapture there will be a seven-year tribulation period.

3. At the end of the tribulation Christ will return and set up rule on earth for one thousand years.

4. The thousand year reign of Christ will end with one last battle, and then eternity will be ushered in.

We might picture it like this:

Present Church Age — 7 Year Tribulation — 1000 Year Reign of Christ on Earth — Eternity

Granted, there are variations and many details that could be added, but this is the popular view most simply stated.

The one major flaw of this popular view is that it has been presented as the *clear* teaching of the Bible. In reality it is far from clear (and, in my opinion, far from the teaching of the Bible). Those who have developed and taught this view have no doubt done so with a clear conscience. However, they have had to begin by accepting a certain set of indemonstrable beliefs. They have taken the plain and simple statements of the Scriptures regarding the end times and interpreted them in the poor light of obscure and difficult texts. This interpreting process in any other area of teaching would bring their stinging rebuke, and rightly so. With this in mind, we must frequently test our own conclusions to see if what we believe is truly in the Bible or just the "traditions of men."

Objectivity – The Importance of being Earnest

It is necessary that the man or woman of God approach the Word of God with a spirit of humility—an attitude that comes to the Word to learn. As you read this booklet it is critical that you take a few moments to assess your own understanding of the end times. How much do you *know* and how firmly do you believe what you know? What do you believe and why? How did you come to your understanding? How might outside influences have affected your conclusions?

In our contemplation of the Lord's return, our concern should not be "what does Dr. Walvoord say?" Or, what does Mr. Rosenthal, Mr. Bray, our pastor, or Sunday school teacher say? Rather, our concern needs to be what does the Bible say? What does God say?

The purpose here is not to intimate that those who have differing views have not been objective; I do want to point out the necessity of objectivity. The Bible student must approach the Bible much in the same way that a good scientist approaches a subject. It has been said that a scientist never tries to prove anything; he only attempts to discover facts. As Christians God calls us to lay aside our preconceived notions so that we may discover what He has to say to us personally. This is often referred to as *inductive* Bible study, reading the Bible to let it speak to us. *Deductive* Bible study is what commonly takes place within the context of a cult. In deductive study the student forms an idea (possibly even a true one!) and then seeks support from the Bible to prove that idea. Inductive study sees the truth presented first and then formulates principles and practices as a result of the discoveries.

While most of us realize the impossibility of total objectivity, I believe it is within the grasp of the believer to be *adequately* objective. It can be exceedingly difficult at times. The pastor who departs from the creed of his church might lose a career in the ministry. The layperson whose conclusions differ from doctrine of the church may lose a desirable position within the structure of that church. Those of us who have little more to lose than ego will find it somewhat easier to be objective. Although it can be humbling to lay aside long held ideas, it can also be rewarding.

Chapter Two

A Biblical Alternative

I believe that the biblical view of the final days is explicitly clear, even though there are some perplexing texts. We have no right to alter the clear texts because we do not understand the problematic passages. Many difficult passages are open to various interpretations, as we shall see later.

I believe that in regard to the final days there is actually only *one* day. I call this view the *One Day* view. I would not suggest that it is a literal twenty-four hour period, but instead of the final events being spread over a one thousand and seven-year period they actually transpire in a relatively short period of time. I believe the Scriptures present this culmination of events as a *day*. I believe that there is but *one* last "day." That day shall begin with the "sound of a trump,"[1] and then the Lord Jesus will descend in burning glory with His angelic hosts and the souls of the departed saints.[2] As He descends, He will shout a loud command and at the sound of His voice all of the dead throughout the earth will rise for judgment.[3]

This judgment begins with the resurrection of the saints and their rescue (via *rapture*) from a doomed people and planet.[4] During (or prior to) our ascension to be with Christ, our bodies will be transformed and made suitable for habitation in the new heavens and new earth.[5] The judgment of the saints results in either rewards or the loss of rewards.[6]

The judgment of sinners will begin as they perish when the old heavens and earth are dissolved by fire.[7] After their resurrection and judgment as individuals takes place, they will be cast into the lake of fire prepared for the devil and his angels.[8] In conjunction with the destruction of the heavens and the earth and the condemnation of sinners, we see the destruction of all the evil dominions, powers, and authorities.[9] Lastly then, death itself is destroyed and thrown into the eternal fire.[10]

Then after the destruction of all evil, God will establish a new heaven and a new earth, the home of righteousness.[11] At that time the Son will turn the Kingdom over to the Father,[12] God will be all in all,[13] and the mystery of God will be finished![14]

Granted, there is much that could be said about each of these events, but the Scripture speaks clearly when it is allowed to do so. The careful reader cannot help but note that the Bible says there will be a last trump, and that, when it sounds, it means "time is up!" The first New Testament mention of this trump is Matthew 24:31.

> *"And he will send his angels with a loud trumpet call, and they will gather his elect from the four winds, from one end of the heavens to the other."*

Now it is *possible* that this text refers to some other event, but it seems to me a reader normally would suppose it refers to a culminating event. However we have other passages that are just as explicitly clear. Take for instance 1 Corinthians 15:51-52.

A Biblical Alternative

> *Listen, I tell you a mystery: We will not all sleep, but we will all be changed –in a flash, in the twinkling of an eye, at the last trumpet. For the trumpet will sound, the dead will be raised imperishable, and we will be changed.*

This passage clearly speaks of a *last* trumpet and the events that occur when it is sounded. The text says when this trumpet sounds, what we call the *rapture* will take place. This clearly indicates that there will be no more trumpets blasted (or how could it be the *last* trumpet?). This does not seem to leave room for more trumpets during a supposed tribulation period, or *another* final trumpet at the end of another one thousand years. All we have to do is turn to 1 Thessalonians 4:16-17 and we can see this same emphasis:

> *For the Lord himself will come down from heaven, with a loud command, with the voice of the archangel and with the trumpet call of God, and the dead in Christ will rise first. After that, we who are still alive and are left will be caught up together with them in the clouds to meet the Lord in the air. And so we will be with the Lord forever.*

There are those who would tell us that we do not understand these verses properly, but it is hard for me to understand why anyone would want them to say anything other than what they seem to say. Although I would agree that Revelation is perhaps the most perplexing book in the Bible, parts of it seem exceedingly clear, parts such as chapter 10, verses 6 and 7.

> *And he swore by him who lives for ever and ever, who created the heavens and all that is in them, the earth and all that is in it, and the sea and all that is in it, and said, "There will be no more delay! But in the days when the seventh angel is about to sound his trumpet, the mystery of God will be accomplished, just as he announced to his servants the prophets."*

It would appear that the seventh trumpet of Revelation is the last trump of the rest of the New Testament. Note what occurs when the trumpet spoken of in the previous verses is sounded:

> *The seventh angel sounded his trumpet, and there were loud voices in heaven, which said: "The kingdom of the world has become the kingdom of our Lord and of his Christ, and he will reign for ever and ever." (Revelation 11:15)*

The verses following the preceding passage reveal to us that the time had come (as a result of the sounding of the trumpet) to reward the saints and to condemn the sinners (see verses 17 and 18). So, we see this order revealed 1) the sounding of the last trumpet, 2) the Lord raising the dead and "rapturing" the saints, 3) the judgment of saints and sinners, and 4) the

A Biblical Alternative

destruction of the old heavens and earth and the establishment of a new heavens and earth.

Part Two

Understanding Hermeneutics

"Do you understand what you are reading?"

Acts 8:30

Chapter Three

The Dangers of Literalism: Turning Bread into Stones

I agree with the old divine who said, "If the literal sense makes good sense seek no other sense lest it result in nonsense!" Those who call themselves *literalists* sometimes intimate that they have some spiritual advantage because of their claim. But they frequently take greater liberties when interpreting the Scripture than those whom they regard as guilty of *spiritualizing* the sacred text. The simple truth is that anyone who reads the Word of God must discern between what is intended to be taken literally and what is to be taken figuratively. If we cannot discern then we should simply say so and lay aside our personal convictions until we gain the needed understanding.

As Christians, our goal is not to be *literal* or *spiritual* (in our interpretation) but rather to be *biblical*. A *biblical* understanding will sometimes be literal and sometimes figurative. If we fail to interpret a passage correctly, then we have turned what God intended to be bread into stones.

If we overhear someone commenting that he or she has some hot news tip that will "shake a town right to the ground" we would not normally think that they are talking about an earthquake (though that is a possibility). We know that they are speaking figuratively and that there is some scandal in the air. Jesus is referred to as the sun in the Bible (Malachi 4:2; Luke 1:78), but few would take this literally! The question, by and large, is one of fairness, since both sides do interpret some portions literally and others figuratively.

The focus must be on where we draw the line as we interpret a statement to be either literal or symbolic. For instance, it does not seem fair for the dispensationalist to refer to Satan's chain in Revelation as anything other than a literal chain if they insist that the thousand years must be a literal thousand years. Nor is it fair to act as though a person *believes* the Bible more because he believes it to be *literally* true. All the great men and women of God believe the Bible to be entirely true. Those who have depth of understanding acknowledge that it is not to be understood without the insight given by the Holy Spirit. If the Bible were merely a *literal* book with a *literal* meaning, then men and women of the world could read and understand all that it contains. But it is more; it is a spiritual book. God Himself tells us that without His Spirit we cannot understand its meaning.[15] Its meaning often transcends a strict literal interpretation.

The primary thing that needs to be understood at this point is that there is actually little difference in the way evangelicals *generally* interpret Scripture. By and large, we use the same rules, and most of the time our differences are minor (in the overall scheme of things). To accuse one another of a wrong hermeneutic is only part of the problem. We are all subject to misinterpreting certain passages. I do not believe that anyone who loves the Lord would *knowingly* misinterpret a passage; ignorantly yes, knowingly, probably not. Our problem is deeper; it relates to the attitude with which we approach our studies. In our next chapter we will attempt to define this more clearly.

Chapter Four

Isolating the Presuppositions

It is my belief that if we go back far enough we can begin to discover why a person holds a particular view on a subject. Perhaps, in the church they grew up in there was only one view taught, and possibly other views were even ridiculed. Maybe since conversion their ideas were unduly influenced by well meaning teachers. It could be through books read, or programs listened to, or watched. I have yet to meet anyone who, in my opinion, could have (or would have!) come up with such a cumbersome position and understanding of the end times as is presented by those who hold to the popular view. I cannot believe that any one individual could sit down with the Scripture and arrive at the positions that it has taken many men nearly two hundred years to develop. I can see where a person might believe in a future millennium by a cursory reading of Revelation 20:1-6. But I question whether a person would conceive the multiple returns, resurrections, and all the ramifications that these events would require.

It is fairly easy to trace the history of the popular view as it has developed over the last two centuries. Briefly, the idea of a "two stage" return was first entertained (as far as I can determine) by a Jesuit Catholic, Manuel Lacunza, in the late 1700s. That such a view can be traced back only this far is quite interesting. His work, *The Coming of the Messiah in Glory and Majesty*, was not published until after his death in the early 1800s. Shortly after its publication it was translated into English by Edward Irving, the forerunner of the Charismatic movement.

One Day

I find it fascinating (even though perhaps irrelevant) that both the Charismatic movement (as we know it today) and the popular view of Christ's return can be traced back to Edward Irving (in particular to events surrounding his parishioner, Miss Margaret McDonald). Enter J.N. Darby, influential leader in the Brethren Movement and an acquaintance of both Irving and the relevant parishioner. Mr. Darby became the first to regard the church age as a "parenthesis" in God's program. Mr. Darby developed and taught his views during his trips to the United States.

These views were then picked up by C. I. Scofield, who incorporated them into the Scofield Reference Bible. From there this view was widely taught and believed primarily because of the popularity of this Bible. Many evangelical scholars disagreed with his views and often parted company with him over them. But the Scofield Bible continued to rise in popularity. The use of such a reference Bible in mainstream evangelical circles eventually had an impact on mainstream preachers, teachers, Bible schools and seminaries. Today this view continues to be propagated via all types of mass media, from popular Christian magazines, book publishers, movie producers, and television evangelists.

With this brief history in mind we need to ask why it is still such a popular view today. I believe it is because it is built on certain presuppositions. As long as a person accepts the presuppositions they do not see a major problem with the conclusions.

It is a difficult job to discover anyone else's presuppositions. As nearly as I can discern, the popular view's first presupposition is that there is a gap (which they call the

Isolating the Presuppositions

parenthesis or *church age*) between the 69th week and the 70th week of Daniel (Daniel 9:24-27). In the next chapter I will try to show why such as idea is totally unwarranted by the Scripture. A house of straw has been built on this presupposition. Based on this passage some people now assume that there is a seven-year period yet in the future for the Jewish race in particular to be blessed by God. By inserting a "church age" (of unknown duration) and teaching the church's departure (via rapture) prior to Daniel's 70th week, they have seven years (not to mention the thousand years!) to insert many passages of Scripture that do not belong in that period.

In the next three chapters we will look at the three primary passages often referred to by those holding to the popular view. Insights will be offered, and questions posed to those willing to look at their view in depth. We will try to isolate the presuppositions and offer a more biblical viewpoint.

Part Three

Relevant Passages

They received the message with great eagerness and examined the Scriptures every day....

Acts 17:11

Chapter Five

Discovering Daniel's Diamond

As we observed in the last chapter, one of the primary presuppositions of the popular view arises from the understanding of the book of Daniel. Those who hold to the popular view believe that when Daniel prophesied about 70 weeks, he was referring to a period of 69 weeks (483 years) followed by a gap of 2000 years or so, and *then* the 70th week, or 7 years. This is certainly not in keeping with a *literal* interpretation. Before we proceed, let's look at the passage as it is given to us in the book of Daniel.

> *Therefore, consider the message and understand the vision:*
>
> *"Seventy 'sevens' are decreed for your people and your holy city to finish the transgression, to put an end to sin, to atone for wickedness, to bring in everlasting righteousness, to seal up vision and prophecy and to anoint the most holy.*
>
> *"Know and understand this: From the issuing of the decree to restore and rebuild Jerusalem until the Anointed One, the ruler, comes, there will be seven 'sevens,' and sixty two 'sevens.' It will be rebuilt with streets and a trench, but in*

> *times of trouble. After the sixty two 'sevens,' the Anointed One will be cut off and will have nothing. The people of the ruler who will come will destroy the city and the sanctuary. The end will come like a flood: War will continue until the end, and desolations have been decreed. He will confirm a covenant with many for one 'seven.' In the middle of the 'seven' he will put an end to sacrifice and offering. And on the wing of the temple he will set up an abomination that causes desolation, until the end that is decreed is poured out on him."*
> *(Daniel 9:23-27)*

While recognizing that Daniel's prophecies are complex and problematic for the most astute student of God's Word, it is my view that the most simple and accurate understanding of the 70 weeks views them as consecutive, without any gaps. To try and place a "parenthesis" or church age between the 69th and 70th weeks is to distort the plain meaning of the passage. The breakdown of weeks is for the purpose of marking time. Besides serving as a chronological guide to the Old Testament, it also helped the Jews of that time to recognize the time of Messiah's coming. This is, in part, how those who were the called of God knew that the time had come for the Messiah to appear.

If I were to tell you that to get to Coos Bay, Oregon from Seattle, Washington you drive south on I-5 until you get to Oregon, then you cut across to Highway 101 and travel south until you see the North Bend bridge, and the next place you come to after North Bend will be Coos Bay, then I have given you unmistakable instructions for locating and recognizing Coos Bay. How could I expect you to understand it otherwise? But what if I *insert* 500 miles between North Bend and Coos Bay? You would end up in San Francisco! And that is the very point. If you insert 2000 years (plus or minus) between the 69th and 70th weeks of Daniel's prophecy you will also end up somewhere other than where you were meant to be! The most satisfying answer comes when we realize that God was not playing games when He told Daniel what to expect and when to expect it. The clearest conclusions come when we read the passage and allow it to speak for itself. Where, I ask, is the *basis* for inserting a gap between the 69th and 70th weeks?

Those who hold the popular view not only misinterpret the length of the 70 weeks (by entertaining a gap notion), but they frequently misinterpret what the Bible clearly teaches about the *beginning* of the 70 weeks as well! The passage above clearly states that the 70 weeks would *begin* with a decree to restore and rebuild Jerusalem. It would appear that the only decree that meets these criteria was issued by Cyrus, and is recorded for us in 2 Chronicles 36:22-23:

> *In the first year of Cyrus king of Persia, in order to fulfill the word of the Lord spoken by Jeremiah, the LORD moved the heart of Cyrus king of Persia to make a proclamation throughout his realm and to put it in writing:*
>
> *"This is what Cyrus King of Persia says:*

> *"The LORD, the God of heaven, has given me all the kingdoms of the earth and he has appointed me to build a temple for him at Jerusalem in Judah. Anyone of his people among you—may the LORD his God be with him, and let him go up."*

Ezra 1:1-4 reiterates this same truth. Jeremiah had revealed that the time of the captivity was to be 70 years, and at the end of 70 years, Israel would return to Judah. Isaiah goes so far as to reveal to us the *name* of the one who would issue this decree. We note especially Isaiah 44:28:

> *"[God] says of Cyrus, 'He is my shepherd and will accomplish all that I please; he will say of Jerusalem, "Let it be rebuilt," and of the temple, "Let its foundations be laid."'"*

The careful student of the Bible can hardly fail to recognize the beginning point of the 70 weeks. Why then do the pre-tribulational, pre-millennial commentators point to some other decree about which Scripture is silent? Perhaps it is primarily because they use a *secular chronology* and go backwards to fit Bible events into it, rather than using the chronology of the Scripture. Those who would like to look deeper into the starting point of the 70 weeks (especially in regard to the Bible's chronology) would be well-advised to read *The Seventy Weeks and the Great Tribulation* by Philip Mauro.[16] The beginning point of Daniel's 70 weeks has been established as the decree of Cyrus by the Scriptures. Those who fail to perceive or believe this will have to turn to secular historians for dates and events to arrive at a starting point.

The first period discussed in the prophecy concerns the events that would take place in the first seven sevens. It is during this period that we read Jerusalem was to be rebuilt...

> "...with streets and a trench, but in times of trouble." (Daniel 9:25)

One can hardly read through Ezra and Nehemiah and not realize how literally these words were fulfilled! To argue that Cyrus' decree was to rebuild a temple and not the city is frivolous, since a thorough reading of the passages gives us the clear indication that they did indeed rebuild their homes as they were rebuilding the temple.

The next period of sevens, the "sixty two sevens," told the people when to expect the Messiah to be revealed! After the decree of Cyrus, they could count out 69 sevens until the Messiah would be revealed. I believe that this passage is, at least in part, why the Jewish women at time of Christ's birth were hopeful of being the mother of the Messiah. They understood that it was near the time when He was to appear. I believe, also, that Simeon, who was "waiting for the consolation of Israel," understood that he was living towards the end of the 69 weeks. God made him a special promise that, although he was apparently old, he would not die before he witnessed the Messiah's coming (Luke 2:25-26).

Now we come to the 70th week, which very naturally follows the 69th week, for those readers who do not project a gap between them. It is during this 70th week that Daniel's vision becomes very specific.

It is in this last week that we see the fulfillment of events prophesied in Daniel 9:24. The first facet of this prophetic diamond pertains to *finishing the transgression*. This was done when Israel crucified the Lord Jesus Christ. Jesus had told the Jewish leaders to "Fill up, then, the measure of the sin of your forefathers" (Matthew 23:32). They did.

The second facet was *to put an end to sin*. The obvious sense of this phrase has to do with the remedy for sin found in the atoning death of Christ. He was a sacrifice for sins, once for all (Hebrews 9:26; 10:12).

A third facet was that, in the 70 weeks, *atonement for wickedness* would be made. What was accomplished through the death of Christ was the availability of reconciliation (2 Corinthians 5:19).

Another facet was that the 70 weeks were to usher in *everlasting righteousness*. I see the manifestation of the Kingdom of God, which Christ ushered in, as being the fulfillment of this.

Fifth, we're told that *prophecy and vision were to be sealed*. There are other interpretations with as much credibility, but I feel this refers to the fact that the prophecies regarding the Messiah were to be fulfilled, or sealed, during His life on earth (Luke 24:44).

Finally, the last facet of our diamond says that in this time frame *the anointing of the most holy* would take place. This could refer to the anointing that took place at Jesus' baptism (Matthew 3:16), or to the coming of the Holy Spirit at Pentecost to consecrate His new temple, the church (Acts 2:1-4), or to Christ's "entering the true tabernacle, which is in heaven, with his own blood" (Hebrews 9:11-12).

Regardless of how we interpret each of these aspects of the prophecy, it is relatively easy to see that they were all centered around, and easily found their fulfillment in, the manifestation of the Messiah. The Cross shines through all the facets of this spiritual gemstone. It is evident that all of these events took place in that 70th week.

The last two verses of our prophecy (Daniel 9:27-28) go even further to enlighten our understanding of the passage, when we compare them with our New Testament understanding. We gain further insight into the meaning of these verses when we see how they are interpreted in the Septuagint (the Greek translation of the Old Testament). The English translation of that version reads:

> *"And one week shall establish the covenant with many; and in the midst of the week my sacrifice and drink offering shall be taken away; and upon the temple shall be the abomination of desolation; and at the end of the time an end shall be put to desolation."*

The basic thought here is that *in* that last week the Messiah would confirm the covenant, putting an end to the old sacrificial system. Then that physical temple would be left desolate, and this would culminate in the end of the Jewish *age*. For a more thorough and fascinating study of these verses, I again recommend Mauro's work on Daniel's 70 weeks.

   The primary point of this chapter is that there is no basis for projecting a supposed gap of 2000 years (or any other period of time) between the 69th and 70th weeks of Daniel. The passage makes good sense if we allow it to be interpreted in a natural manner. All of the prophecies that were made were beautifully fulfilled in the coming of the promised Messiah. With this in mind why would anyone want to regard these prophecies as referring to some future *evil* ruler?

Chapter Six

The Olivet Discourse

It is of the utmost importance to note not only the *content*, but the *context*, of the Olivet discourse. Jesus had just finished condemning the *leaders* of the Jewish religion with "seven woes." Next He turns His attention to the *city* of the Jews, Jerusalem. Note carefully the words He uses in Matthew 23:38-39, specifically the phrases

> *"your house is left to you desolate"*

and in verse 39

> *"you will not see me again…."*

I believe that two things would have stood out to the disciples who heard Jesus say these things. First, the term *desolate* would bring to mind Daniel's prophecy regarding the *abomination of desolation*. Second, it didn't sound as if Jesus intended to reappear in Jerusalem anytime soon. As they then leave the city the disciples point out to Jesus the grandeur of the temple, which to them represented the power of the Jewish system. It would be much like us being in awe at the sight of the Mormon Temple in Salt Lake City. Even though we believe it represents an evil system, we do not believe it will be readily dissolved. Jesus told the disciples that the Temple that they are so impressed with would be leveled to the ground! After the disciples listened to Jesus lambasting the Jewish leaders, pitying the Holy City, and promising the destruction of the Holy Temple, would they not somehow connect His return with that destruction? I think so, as we shall see.

After the Lord and His disciples arrived at the Mount of Olives, a group of His followers came forward to ask him about His previous comments. When you and I read His response some 2000 years later we are apt to try and make their questions fit into our thinking. Attempt to look at it from the first disciples' point of view. They did not, at this point, understand the nature of Jesus' mission (His death, burial, resurrection, and ascension). They were not inquiring as to the time of His return with the angels to judge the earth. They simply wanted to know when He would be going back to Jerusalem to level the Temple and usher in His new rule. They wanted to know "when is all of this going to take place?" The disciples asked this question from an earthly point of view. They thought that the overthrow of Rome was just around the corner. The Lord's response was one that scanned time and eternity and placed events in their proper perspective.

Jesus began with the impending event, the destruction of Jerusalem, the leveling of the temple, *the end of the Jewish age*! Before it would happen, Jesus said in Matthew 24 that they would see:

1. False Christs (v. 5)
2. Wars and news of wars (v. 6)
3. Famines and earthquakes (v. 7)

Jesus said these events were only the beginning. Things would get worse. There would be:

4. Persecution of the saints (v. 9)

5. The love of most would grow cold (v. 12)

And then before the end of the age Jesus said:

6. The Gospel would be preached to all nations (v. 14)

In other words, things would look worse and worse to the disciples, and then they would see Jerusalem surrounded by armies, *the abomination of desolation*! Jesus told them what to do at that time:

a) If you live in Judea head for the hills (v. 16)

b) Ignore the false messiahs (v. 23)

The period from the discourse of Jesus to the actual destruction of Jerusalem was around 35 to 40 years, or about a generation. All of these things that took place fulfilled the predictions of Jesus in this passage.

Josephus, the first century historian, documents that all of these things did indeed take place during the destruction of Jerusalem. It is not possible, nor does it make good sense, to demand that the events in Matthew 24:29-31 were also fulfilled in the apostolic age. Granted, a cursory reading might demand such an interpretation. There *are* schools of thought that teach that all of these events were fulfilled historically. But the Son of God has *not yet* come on the clouds of heaven. Any attempt to explain that this part of the text was fulfilled in 70 A.D. seems a bit far-fetched. The language used here regarding our Lord's return is consistent with the rest of the New Testament teaching. A preferable interpretation, in my mind, would go along these lines:

- Verses 4-13 refer to the events that would precede the end of the age. What age? The age the disciples were inquiring about in verse 3. It is most probable that they were referring to the "Jewish Age" or the age of the Law.

- Verses 15-25 speak about the destruction of Jerusalem itself and the end of the age.

- Verses 26-28 are a reiteration of earlier verses (4, 5, 23), reminding the disciples not to look for Christ's appearance at that time. Only false Christs would appear on the scene. When Jesus returns, it will *not* be in secret!

- Verses 29 and following form an important transition. I believe that Jesus is telling the disciples what it will be like *after* the end of the age, *until* His final return.

With this interpretation in mind, when Jesus said, "This generation will certainly not pass away until all these things have happened" (v. 34), it seems He was referring not to the events of verses 29-31, but to the events of verses 4-25.

R.C. Sproul writes that the Greek words translated "all of these things" could easily refer to the destruction of the Temple and Jerusalem.[17] While this interpretation of the Olivet discourse may not be popularly received, it is nonetheless a very plausible explanation of the passage.

Chapter Seven

Reveling In Revelation

Once, during my years in the counter-culture living on a commune, I sat with a couple of friends and proceeded to read to them the book of Revelation. After listening to about twelve chapters, they politely excused themselves. No doubt it conjured up wild images in our drugged minds. It was beyond our understanding! That was over thirty five years ago, and though I haven't touched an illegal drug since then, have graduated from Bible College, and have read and studied Revelation many times, in many ways it is still beyond my understanding! I do not deny it, nor do I ignore it.

A good portion of what has been written about the book of Revelation has far more to do with speculation than interpretation. Invariably a commentator begins with a great promise to enlighten the reader. Certainly each author has some valid points and observations, but most of the authors I have read offer no genuine clarification of the contents of the book—only *guesses*!

Revelation is a difficult book to understand. It is a little like the man who named his dog Revelation. When he was asked why he said, "Because I don't understand it but I love it anyway!" Revelation is a sobering book. It takes us through the sufferings of the church and into the glories of the eternal state. It reveals the glory of God and His Son Jesus Christ and their ultimate conquest over sin and the evil forces in the world. Revelation speaks to us of a risen Christ, who interacts with the saints and promises us both a resurrection

One Day

and a judgment. I believe that much of Revelation is incomprehensible to our modern thinking. Perhaps the early believers, to whom the book was first addressed, had greater insight into the symbolic language that was used.

Let the reader forget all of the *systems* and *interpretations* previously learned, take pen and paper in hand, and come up with an order of events and understanding. Soon, I believe, the honest student will give in and say "it is beyond my ability." This is the starting place for learning—to acknowledge ignorance. Now the thinking can begin. Now we can subject our thinking to Word of God rather than the traditions of men. It is unfortunate that in our world well-organized ignorance often passes for wisdom! I suggest that we let God speak to us through Revelation and quit trying to arrange and rearrange the Bible to fit our thinking. Perhaps, just perhaps, Revelation is meant to help us revel in the grace of an incomprehensible God, instead of satisfying our curiosity about the details of the end time.

Seven Seals, Seven Trumpets

As I was preparing this booklet, I asked a friend if there was any area of prophecy that he felt especially should be addressed. He said he'd like to hear my views on the seven seals and seven trumpets of Revelation. Knowing that I believed the "great tribulation" was historically fulfilled, he could not comprehend how I could understand such great catastrophes as having taken place historically. I would, in all honesty, have to say that perhaps such catastrophes have not taken place historically. Maybe they will take place in the future. Even so, I do not see them fitting into a future seven year "tribulation period." Some or all of these seals and/or trumps may yet be future to us and still not be a part of what the dispensationalists call a "tribulation."

It is interesting to me that pre-tribulationists make so much of events that they don't believe they will be around during anyway! The first thing that I would note regarding the seals and trumpets is that their context in Revelation gives us no hint as to their timing in history, other than the fact they were to occur after Jesus had ascended into heaven (see 5:9-14) and prior to His return to usher in eternity (see 11:15-19). The context might actually *hint* that the first seal was opened when Jesus first returned to heaven.

Reading through the seven seals, we get the impression that they take place in quick succession. I think John was giving us his general impressions of what was taking place in the visions the Lord gave him, and not striving to be exacting in his proportions. Much of what he says is perhaps to be taken figuratively. Pre-millennialists who take chapter 6:12-14 literally must explain how a thousand-year reign of peace and joy will take place on a planet that has just been nearly annihilated! No doubt God could repair the planet, but there is no hint in Scripture of a new heaven and a new earth until eternity is ushered in!

At the sounding of the seventh trump in chapter 11:15, we see the consummation of all things, the Day of Judgment. The context gives no hint of a millennial reign following this day. Nor does it seem that the first six trumpets could have occurred during the brief span of a theoretical tribulation period while the seventh would not be blown until the end of some thousand year reign of Christ! I do not claim to know without question when the seals and trumpets take place in the course of history. Who can say with certainty what these things mean and when they occur?

The Binding of Satan in Revelation 20 or "Two half hitches and a square knot"

My granddad used to say that "two half hitches and a square knot would hold the devil." While it is doubtful that rope could hold Satan it is probably just as doubtful that a literal chain would hinder him. A chain does not necessarily keep a person from moving about; however it does restrict the area of movement. Revelation 20 tells us that Satan has been "bound" since the time of Christ's death and resurrection, that is his power is now restrained.

Jesus said He saw Satan fall from heaven like lightning (Luke 10:18). First Peter tells us that the devil is prowling around like a roaring lion, looking for someone to devour.[18] Do not these two truths together hint to us that there is a sense in which the devil's work is now limited to the sphere of the earth?

The premillennialist may respond, "Doesn't the Bible teach us that Satan is the god or ruler of this age?" (see 2 Corinthians 4:4). Yes, but 1 John 4:4 tells us that greater is He that is in us than *He* that is in the world (that is the devil). Christ has now conquered Satan. He is "bound," he is on "death row," but he is still alive and powerful. He roams the earth, and he rules the unsaved (1 John. 5:19). Only the Christian who is walking with God is "out of his reach".

Satan's binding does not necessitate the destruction of his power, only the limitation of it. Colossians 2:15 tells us that Christ triumphed over the "powers and authorities" (that is the devil and his demons), and yet, we see that prior to their final execution they will be loosed (Revelation 20:7). This binding is said to be for a thousand years. I do not believe it is to be taken literally anymore than when the Bible teaches us that God owns the cattle on a thousand hills, or that an earthly day is no different than a thousand years for the Lord (2 Peter 3:8). All these uses of "one thousand" are just a manner of speaking, like "I've told you a thousand times!"

I think that the "thousand years" of Revelation 20 is indicative of the period when Satan was first bound until he is freed, shortly before the Second Coming. At this point his power will be felt in ways that perhaps it never was before. We may be seeing a beginning of this in our day, through the evil use of electronic mass media. When he is "loosed," Satan's power will be unrestrained until the Lord Jesus comes to destroy him and usher in eternity.

Another basic presupposition of the popular view seems to be that these teachers think that they can and do understand the book of Revelation. Many people trust their teachers and simply reiterate what they have been taught without actually gaining their own understanding.

In the next section we will look at some of the key terms and concepts that those who hold to the popular view frequently refer to, and we will offer some alternative explanations.

Part Four

Terms and Concepts

"What is truth?"

John 18:38

Chapter Eight

"Ages"

In the Bible an "age" is a period of time characterized by some event or events that separate it from another period of time. In Jewish thinking, there were "ages" past (see Ephesians 3:9; Romans 16:25; Colossians 1:26). Probably, in their thinking, there was an *age* prior to the flood, an *age* of Egyptian captivity, an *age* of the Exodus, and so on. *Ages*, in this sense, are somewhat relative. It is in the same sense as we speak of the age of enlightenment, the space age, the new age, and so on. While there may be some areas of overlap, we normally understand what the speaker means by the context of the statements.

Jesus referred, basically, to two ages. He spoke of the *present age*, and the *next age*, that is eternity. We learn from the New Testament that Satan is the god of this age (2 Corinthians 4:4); it is an evil age (Galatians 1:4), and yet Christ promises to be with us to the end of the age (Matthew 28:19, 20).

When Jesus referred to "the age to come", He said that there would be a harvest to usher it in (Matthew 13:39, 40, 49).

There does seem to be a third *age* to which the Lord referred. In Matthew 24 He promised the disciples the sign of a destroyed temple to signal the end of the Jewish religious institution. This would also help us to see how the sin against the Holy Spirit could be unforgivable in that age or the age to come (that would be either in the Jewish age or the Christian age).

  Regardless of how one views the various ages, it is difficult to see how we could possibly insert a millennial *age* into the teaching of Christ. He did not mention a millennial age prior to the harvest and the ushering in of eternity. When Christ spoke of the ages, it was with finality and decisiveness. He was living in a sense in two ages, the Jewish age (of which He could see the end), and the Christian age (which He ushered in). He anticipated and taught only one more age as nearly as I can discern, the age to come—eternity.

> *Great and marvelous are your deeds, Lord God Almighty. Just and true are your ways, King of the ages. (Revelation 15:3)*

Chapter Nine

Everything You Wanted to Know about the Antichrist (but were afraid to ask!)

The term *antichrist* is found only five times in the Bible (all references are in First and Second John). What we learn about the antichrist from the apostle John's first epistle can be summarized as follows:

1. There was *an* antichrist coming, even though many antichrists had already come (2:18).
2. The antichrist would be a *person* who would deny the Father and the Son (2:22).
3. The *spirit* of the antichrist existed prior to his personal appearance (4:3).

Second John refers to antichrist only one time and tells us one significant fact: *anyone* who does not acknowledge Jesus as having come in the flesh is the antichrist (v.7).

In both books we see a person referred to as *the* antichrist. First John seems to portray an individual sort of antichrist that we have come to expect today (whether or not we should).[19] Second John seems to indicate that really any person (or group?) could equally be considered *the* antichrist. Translators and commentators do not agree that these verses need be interpreted as *the* antichrist. It could well be that John was not pointing to a single person.

It appears to me that everything that we can *know* about antichrist is confined to what we see in First and Second John. There are other passages that we *assume* refer to the same personage, but we must be careful to understand that we are only assuming (perhaps correctly) that they refer to the same person.

The Man of Lawlessness

> *Don't let anyone deceive you in any way, for that day will not come until the rebellion occurs and the man of lawlessness is revealed, the man doomed to destruction. He will oppose and will exalt himself over everything that is called God or is worshiped, so that he sets himself up in God's temple, proclaiming himself to be God. (2 Thessalonians. 2:3, 4)*

Here in 2 Thessalonians, the apostle Paul refers to an individual that many also call the antichrist. He informs us that prior to the Lord's return a man will appear who will exalt himself and proclaim himself to be God. He will be a man who performs counterfeit miracles, signs, and wonders.

A study done by John Bray reveals that the temple spoken of in this passage was not the temple then in existence at Jerusalem, or the temple that many expect to see built in the future.[20] The word used for temple here is *naos* and, according to the *Theological Dictionary of the New Testament*,[21] while it could refer to a physical temple it more likely refers to the church as the temple of the Holy Spirit, the body of Christ. This antichrist was someone who would infiltrate the church of

Christ, God's temple. He will be destroyed by the Lord at His glorious coming. The inference here is that there will be an individual who most certainly is *an* antichrist (and in the sense of Second John *the* antichrist).

It is worth noting here that Paul's message is very clear to the Thessalonians: they don't need to worry about missing the coming of the Lord. It will not occur until after a certain event, that is the manifestation of the man of sin. It is odd that those who seem most concerned about the man of sin appearing on the scene today are those who teach that the coming of the Lord will *precede* his appearance! This teaching is quite contrary to Paul's teaching on the subject. Paul says that before that great and glorious coming of our Lord (at which we will be gathered unto Him), the man of lawlessness will have been revealed. Before he can be revealed, however, there is some force or power that must be removed, something that holds him back. The popular teaching is that this force is the Holy Spirit, and it is the removal of the church that allows the antichrist to be made manifest. This appears to me to be exactly opposite of what the passage is trying to teach us. While it is evident that we do not know what force keeps the man of sin from being revealed, our comfort should be the same as was given to the Thessalonians—that we will not miss the day of the Lord. On that final day we will not only discover who or what the antichrist is, we will also observe the destruction of the antichrist.

Elementary, My Dear Watson

From the texts we have observed so far, we can understand that there will be antichrists until the very end, and that one of these antichrists (whom we could label The Antichrist) will be manifested *prior* to the Lord's return.

Revelation – Speculation

Some also speculate that it is this same antichrist that is spoken of in Revelation 13:1-8 and 19:20. It is possible, perhaps even probable, that such is the case, but it is less clear than the above quoted passages. Let us be content to say this is another passage that appears to refer to the same person, rather than making it a mark of orthodoxy that all must agree upon.

If indeed this is the same entity as the antichrist of First John and Second Thessalonians, then we see that he does not act alone, but has a "right hand man." He has a prophet who serves him, a *false* prophet who acts on his behalf.

Revelation 13:15 infers that it is only those who know the Lord who do not serve these two. In Thessalonians it is the antichrist who performs signs, miracles, and wonders, while here in Revelation, it is a second party who performs them on behalf of another party.

Expositors throughout the centuries have come up with numerous theories about the nature and person of the Antichrist. There are many convincing arguments for believing that the papal authority of Roman Catholicism has historically fulfilled such a role perfectly.[22] Others that have been suggested range from the ludicrous to plausible.[23]

It is not *essential* in order to be a godly believer that we interpret the Scripture in such a fashion as to anticipate a *future* manifestation of a personal Antichrist. The criteria have been adequately fulfilled historically so that we cannot make a future appearance an absolute prerequisite to our Lord's return. And yet I would not be adamant that there is no possibility of some future Antichrist.

Regardless of the possibility of a future manifestation of an antichrist, the clear teaching of Scripture seems to be that the world will grow increasingly evil until the very end, when Christ will return triumphantly to destroy the devil and his followers. I believe that much of what is being taught today about an antichrist within the popular prophetic circles is pure speculation. Those who feel Scripture necessitates or warrants a future man of sin must demonstrate how Luther, Calvin, and other notable figures within church history failed in their understanding when they concluded that the Roman Catholic system was the Antichrist.

What then shall we do with the Antichrist? We must be aware of biblical teachings and understand that the text does allow for historical fulfillment (future when it was written, history to us now). If he has appeared historically then there is no other event that must precede our Lord's return. If he has not yet appeared then he must appear before the Lord's descent from heaven to establish the new heavens and new earth. What then shall we do? As we seek further understanding we shall also continue to "live in him, rooted and built up in him, strengthened in the faith…" (Colossians 2:6-7).

Chapter Ten

Kingdom of God or Kingdom of Heaven?

The popular view has also espoused that there is a difference between the kingdom of God and the kingdom of heaven. There *is* a difference—one speaks of the Ruler, and one speaks of the realm. However, this is not the difference that those teaching the popular view propagate in their teaching.

According to the popular view the phrase *Kingdom of God* refers to a spiritual kingdom, that is a kingdom for the church during an "age of grace," while the *Kingdom of heaven* refers to an earthly millennial kingdom offered to the Jews, a kingdom they rejected. The popular view teaches that Jesus offered the Jews a kingdom, but when they rejected that kingdom, God put plan B (the church) into effect.

The major problem with this view is that it is totally unbiblical! Jesus clearly said His kingdom was not of this world (John 18:36). When the Jews *wanted* to make Him king, He went the other way (John 6:15). Jesus did not come to set up an earthly kingdom, nor was His plan in *any way* thwarted. Read through the New Testament's recorded reasons for Jesus' entrance into the world, and you will never find that He came to set up an earthly kingdom for the Jewish people.[24] To read this into the Bible and try to differentiate between the *Kingdom of God* and the *Kingdom of heaven* in such a manner is an irresponsible handling of the word of God.

The terms *kingdom of God* and *kingdom of heaven* are used interchangeably and synonymously. Readers can verify this simply by comparing the parallel passages in the Gospels. Even as a young Christian when I was taught that these phrases referred to different kingdoms, I could never quite accept it. Now I see that it distorts the plain meaning of the Bible and imposes an understanding that the biblical writers never intended. Some leaders who espouse the popular view are changing their views about the use of these terms. That is a step in the right direction.

The popular view has also tweaked other terms that are used interchangeably in the Scripture. They teach that there are differences between the *Day of the Lord,* the *Day of Christ,* and the *Day of God*.[25] They differentiate between the *Judgment seat of Christ* and the *Judgment seat of God*. Such divisions cannot be explained or supported by Scripture unless a person approaches the Bible using the popular view template as a starting point.

Chapter Eleven

The Secret Rapture

The rapture of the church is a cardinal doctrine. It is the blessed hope of every believer (Titus 2:13). However, until the popular view was introduced there was no reason to regard it as a *secret* rapture.

When the rapture takes place the living saints will be caught up in the clouds and the bodies of those that have previously died in Christ will precede those who are still living (1 Thessalonians 4:15-17). The unbelievers who are left behind are those who must now face the punishment of God and be banned for their unbelief. They may not see us *disappear*, but they will see us reappear in our glorified bodies coming with the Lord Jesus and a mighty host of angels! Those who are left behind will not have *another chance* to be saved, but they will be like those who cry out for the rocks to fall on them and save them from the wrath of the Lamb (Luke 23:30; Hebrews 10:31; Revelation 6:15-16).

As the popular view presents the rapture it will be followed by a seven-year period referred to as the tribulation, when people will have another chance to turn to Christ. They teach that living on the earth will not be pleasant during those seven years, but nonetheless they allow that many people will come to the faith. This is an unusual teaching. Nowhere is such a teaching found in the New Testament. That people would have a second chance to be saved after the coming of the Lord Jesus is a violation of every sound principle of biblical interpretation. Jesus warned people to be ready because there would be no second chance (Matthew 24:44-51; 25:1-13). Jesus and the entire New Testament teach that we should be ready for the Lord's return at any time and that His return will be the culminating event of history as we know it. In Acts 3:21 we are told the Lord Jesus will remain in heaven until the time comes for God to restore all things. Those who teach the popular view try to construct a difference between the Lord coming *for* His saints and the Lord coming *with* His saints. This is theological nonsense. The New Testament clearly speaks of a single return of Christ that will bring deliverance for believers and judgment for nonbelievers. To try and make it say otherwise is a compromise of integrity.

Chapter Twelve

The Times of the Gentiles

The phrase *Times of the Gentiles* is a popular one in prophetic circles today. Like many other terms it has been interpreted differently by various commentators. Theodore Epp, a prominent premillennialist, defines the term as the period of time from Nebuchadnezzar's conquest of Jerusalem in 606 B.C. until the Second Coming of Christ. While this *may* be the approximate timeframe and the correct understanding, it should be noted that this is not a term that can be so easily defined. Commentators throughout the ages have disagreed on the meaning of this phrase, which is found only once in the Bible.

> *Jerusalem will be trampled on by the Gentiles until the times of the Gentiles are fulfilled. (Luke 21:24)*

While expositors have made much of this phrase, it would appear that the context itself gives us the best understanding of its meaning. This period could legitimately be described as the period of time when the Gentiles exercise judgment over Jerusalem. Historically this was accomplished when Jerusalem was destroyed by Rome in A.D. 70. Another possible understanding of this term could be that it refers to the time since the cross when the Gentiles have been acknowledged as God's people as much as the Jews. In this sense it would mean that once all those who are called by God to inherit the Kingdom come to Christ, then the culmination of all events will take place. This phrase is neither a basis nor a main point for understanding end time theology. The United Bible Societies' *A Translator's Handbook on the Gospel of Luke*, states, "the exact meaning of the phrase is very uncertain."[26] Often commentators read more into this phrase than is biblically justified in order to embellish their eschatological positions. While I grant that this may be a simplistic perspective, I question anyone who reads into the Bible more than God wants it to say. Let us hold fast to the Word of God, while being very careful with the traditions of men.

Chapter Thirteen

Of Israel and Jews

In certain prophetic circles much is made of Jews and Israel. It has been with much prophetic interest that Israel gained its national status in 1948. Many Bible teachers believe that this is the fulfillment of prophecy and that there will be a great turning of the Jews to Christ. But is this what the Bible teaches? Shall a race of people re-inhabit the land of Israel and turn to Christ? Where is the chapter and verse for such a belief? I believe that there may be a future turning of Jews to Christ as long as we remember that a Jew is a member of a religious group and *not a race*. The real question that the student must ask today, especially in the context of prophecy, is "exactly what is a Jew?" This is a question that demands an answer, and yet it seems few students of prophecy have adequately dealt with this question.

I have pondered and posed this question numerous times and have received various answers. The *Encyclopedia Britannica*,[27] points out that there is no such thing today as a Jewish race. After reading this statement and not finding it mentioned in newer editions, I wrote to the publishers to find out why. In reply I received a very courteous and enlightening response explaining that the newer editions contained new, rewritten, or heavily revised articles. The response also explained that the author of the previously written article on Jews was simply making an observation that Jews do not constitute a race as defined scientifically. This response went even further by quoting from the *Encyclopedia Judaica* to demonstrate that it is difficult for people to comprehend that the Jewish people of today do not constitute a race (a homogeneous group that is easily recognizable) [28]

From an anthropological viewpoint, Jews do not constitute a race. There are basically three races: Negroes, Orientals, and Caucasians. Jews are found in each of these races. There is no single physical characteristic that is common to all Jews. During Hitler's reign of terror there were many non-Jews who were put to death while many Jews were never discovered. Jean-Paul Sartre tells of his friend who was a German Jew. This man used to amuse himself by going out on walks with one of the German officers who bragged that he could "tell a Jew a hundred yards away."

If we are to address further the question of the Jewish race then we must turn to the Bible for our understanding. What does the Bible mean by *race*? The word for race in the Old Testament is *zera* and is usually translated by such other words as *descendants* (82 times), *offspring* (35 times), *seed* (25 times), *child* (20 times), and *family* (5 times). In the New Testament race is from the Greek word *syngenes*, which is also translated as *relative(s)* (10 times). This would seem to make it clear that when the Bible speaks of race it is a little different than when the world speaks of race.

In the Bible a race is a group of people who are all descended from common ancestors. The purity of such a race obviously depends upon the intermarriage that takes place over the years. According to the Bible we all descended from Adam and Eve (Genesis 3:20; Acts 17:26). We are the race of Adam. Over the years people began to draw lines to distinguish themselves. After the flood, for instance, there were three lines drawn. According to my understanding of Scripture,

Of Israel and Jews

everyone today is either from the race of Shem, Ham, or Japeth. As we descended from them no doubt there was intermarriage until all three lines crossed and crisscrossed beyond tracing.

When we speak of Israel in a *racial* sense, we mean all the descendants of one man, *Israel*. Initially it was a fairly pure race, although each of Jacob's sons married outside the house of Israel! They were apparently distinguishable from the Egyptians when they dwelt in Egypt. After the Jews left Egypt they received the Law, which became the basis of their religion. While their race was being diluted with time, religion became the bonding power of these people. Israelites were not supposed to marry outside of their race, but the Old Testament reveals that they often did. Over the centuries many other nationalities were allowed to intermarry with the Jews because they accepted the Jewish faith. Through intermarriage with those who were not descended from Jacob, racial purity was eventually eradicated. Today it would be virtually impossible for a person to demonstrate that he or she actually descended from Jacob.

Most of us would immediately think of King David as a *pure* Jew. We need not look into his genealogy very far to discover that he could not be considered a *racially* pure Jew. His great grandmother was Ruth, the Moabitess, with whom intermarriage was strictly forbidden (Deuteronomy 23:3). His great great grandmother was Rahab, the harlot. Though these women were far from the race of Israel they were considered partakers of the faith of Israel and, in a very real sense, they *became* Jews.[29]

Though the bloodline of Jewish descent weakened over the years, Jews held together because they had a common faith and a common home. They had become a nation. While they were in Egypt they were a people without a land. They had their customs and leaders, but no real freedom or government under the rule of the Egyptians. Now, after the conquest of Canaan, they had government and a land. They were really a nation. They were the *Jewish* nation.

Because a person does not believe in a pure Jewish *race* does not make that person anti-Semitic. We are to love all men the same, regardless of their nationality. If the Jews of today are not a race, what are they? Why do we call certain people "Jews"?

I think we must realize that over the years the term *Jew* has taken on many connotations. *Historically*, it was reserved for those people referred to as Hebrews (though actually this could refer to all of the descendants of *Eber*) or Israelites, the children of Jacob or Israel. This, then, would refer to a *race* of Jews, a race which was "contaminated" from the beginning. Recognizing the intermarriages that have taken place throughout the centuries, it would be difficult to argue for the purity of the Jewish race (or any other race) and impossible to prove. In reality what happened was that the race then developed into a *religion*. In Esther we find the following statement:

> *And many people of other nationalities became Jews because fear of the Jews had seized them. (Esther 8:17)*

Of Israel and Jews

That the Jewish *religion* has existed continually since its inception is without question. Therefore those who have been nurtured in that religion can be and are called "Jews." They are Jewish in the sense that they follow the religion that was given by God to the Jews. That religion was supposed to bring them to Christ. Although the religion still exists today, it is not with God's blessing. True Jews (that is those who were true spiritual children of God) were those who listened to God and accepted the One He sent. Jesus Himself made it clear that just because a person was called a Jew was no indication that he really was a Jew (John 8:39-47). Paul reinforced this message (Romans 9:6-7). It is difficult to think that God would extend special favor today to any group of people or system of beliefs that deny Jesus as the Christ, the Son of God. The Jewish religion today refuses to acknowledge Jesus Christ as the Messiah. If a Jewish person accepts Christ as the Messiah they become a Christian.

Since the race must be regarded as an impure race, and the religion must be regarded as a false religion, we are left with only one other way to define the word *Jew*: those who have chosen to live in Israel and by means of *nationality* are Jewish. I live in United States so I am an American. I could be descended from any race and still be an American. This is just as true in Israel. Blacks, Russians, and Westerners live in Israel. When they become citizens of Israel they might regard themselves as Jews. There is no "proof" that a person is a Jew.

Historically then, we see that the term *Hebrew* referred to numerous Semitic peoples, while in Jewish history it refers to those tribes who accepted Yahweh as God. *Israelite* connotes a particular ethnic and national group descended from the

Hebrews and united culturally by their religion of *Judaism*. The term *Jew* refers to the cultural descendents of the two. To say that there is a Jewish race today would be about as accurate as referring to a Christian race or a hippie race.

To summarize, those who call themselves Jews are not really Jews in the sense of race, *unless* the criteria we use for a race is redefined to mean less than it does in a scientific sense. When we speak of Jews today I believe a good definition would be that they are *a group of people bound together by ancestral heritage and often a quasi belief in the God of Abraham*. I do not believe the Bible teaches a future turning of the Jews to Jesus unless it is understood in a religious sense: specifically that they will give up Judaism to accept Jesus Christ as Lord and Savior.

Part Five

The Conclusion of the Matter

The end of a matter is better than its beginning....

Ecclesiastes 7:8

Chapter Fourteen

What Difference Does It Make?

Does it really matter very much what we believe about the end times? Our belief in one system or another will not change the plans of God, so why all the fuss? What are the ramifications of the popular view?

I believe that it matters what we believe about end times. The Second Coming of Christ is an essential teaching and must not be neglected in our evangelism and discipleship. Of course our beliefs will not change God's plans. The fuss is because if we cannot understand the clear teaching of Scripture on this important subject we have no business teaching others. There is a world of difference between *repeating* explanations and *understanding* explanations. The fuss is because there are many ramifications of our positions.

The popular view has a *few* grave errors that produce their own problems. First, the popular view does not *correctly handle* the Word of God as we are admonished to do in 2 Timothy 2:15. It has taken the KJV phrase "rightly divide" the Word and abused it. According to James 3:1 teachers will be held accountable for such misleading and mishandling of the Word of God. While there are different ages or "dispensations" in the Bible, the proper study of them will not produce what we have come to know today as dispensationalism. Those who accept dispensationalism without investigating and understanding it need to step back and reevaluate what they are doing and why they are doing it. Those who teach without understanding their epistemology need to be reminded that they will be judged more strictly if they endorse and pass on false teaching. Truly this becomes a matter of integrity (Titus 2:1, 7-8).

Secondly, the popular view has ignorantly assumed a cultish tone by isolating and at times even ridiculing those who question their "scheme of things." Those who hold this view seem to feel that their view is *THE* orthodox view, and anyone who does not agree with them is suspect in their own theology. In reality they cannot present an *understanding* of their view. Others simply must accept it without question. This is exactly what non-Christian cults practice: "It is my way or the highway!"

Thirdly, they have made a *very* serious error in teaching people that after the Lord's coming (though they regard it as phase one of a multiple phase return) there will be a second chance to be saved. While I don't believe that this is the intent of their instruction, it is nonetheless an obvious outcome of such teaching. This seems all the more dangerous when we see how they compare the rapture with a thief in the night and yet disregard the context and continuity of such passages as 1 Thessalonians 4:16, 17; 5:2; and 2 Peter 3:10. Jesus Himself offered no one a second chance after His return (Matthew 25:1-13).

Finally, by relegating passages such as the Sermon on the Mount and the Lord's Prayer to a future age they deny that Jesus was instructing the church. I do not think we have too many extreme dispensationists who apply these passages in such a manner, but the system they teach would conclude that they should. Joseph Stowell in his book *Eternity* explains the more common dispensational understanding by commenting

What Difference Does It Make?

that while the material in the Sermon on the Mount is for the millennial reign, it is none the less applicable for us today as well. [30] I cannot help but ask what is so different about the millennial time period if these teachings are primarily for such a time? According to such thinking there will still be injustice, poverty, and persecution for the faith, anger, adultery, divorce, greed, and a host of other problems. What makes the millennial time period different than what we are presently experiencing? And why would people be taught to pray the Lord's Prayer during the millennium (especially "Thy kingdom come")? If we feel that these teachings are for us in a secondary sense rather than in a primary sense, we may not give them the priority that they so richly deserve. Only in recent church history has anyone taught that these passages are not applicable to the present church of Jesus Christ.

If these passages are not applicable directly to the church, which ones are and how is the common Christian to discover how to walk with God? Do we need a priest to translate the plain English Bible for us?

Summary

The dispensational system makes for fine fiction, but we have to be careful to separate fiction from reality. I told my children as they were growing up that they should read the *Left Behind* series as a sort of Christian Science Fiction. As adults we must treat such teaching as either true or false (or as science fiction), or simply acknowledge that we are unable to understand what the Bible teaches in this area. We are acting out of accord with Christianity if we accept any doctrine just because it was taught to us by our pastor or Sunday school teacher! We are to be like the Berean church and e*xamine the Scriptures.*

Chapter Fifteen

A Cloud of Witnesses

I have heard and read many times about men turning from pretribulational/premillennialism to the view proposed here. But I have rarely read or heard of anyone who has studied and turned from this view to the popular view. It has been interesting to hear about great men and women of the past who at first believed pretribulational/premillennialism because of its popularity, but after a time returned to the clear teaching of the Bible.

While many who seek greater understanding change their views, many do not. I would not pass judgment on those who do not change views. I have contemplated this at length, and I feel there are several reasons such people may not change views. One possible reason is that they do not feel the subject is important enough to merit the study that is required to resolve the issues. It is easier to just accept long-held traditional views. While this is not the honorable way out, it is frequently the easy and accepted way. The honorable response would be to admit ignorance and resolve not to take a stance until, or unless, the issues are thoroughly studied.

Some people simply refuse to change views because anyone who questions the long-held view they have been taught is suspect. While it is true that we should be careful to evaluate teaching that is new to us, the fact that it is new does not mean it is not true. Many teachers today would not dare to evaluate this teaching with the objectivity they do the rest of Scripture because if they were to change positions they would be disfellowshipped or dismissed by their congregations or institutions. It is the person who has nothing to lose, or is willing to lose all, who is more apt to treat the study with the respect that it deserves. For this reason this booklet is written for the layperson. Hopefully, it will have a trickle-up effect. That is, if laypeople gain a basic understanding of the issues at hand and gently confront their pastors and teachers with appropriate questions, then we shall perhaps see them reevaluate their positions.

Chapter Sixteen

How Then Shall We Live?

Once in a while someone remarks that the view presented here does not do much to encourage people or to inspire evangelistic zeal. While I cannot say that my eschatological position has made me more zealous for the Lord's work, it certainly leaves no less room for evangelistic fervor. Those of us who hold that the Lord's return is to be soon, and final, actually have *more* reason to be zealous than those who believe that after the rapture people can still come to Christ. We believe when He returns again there will be no more chance for repentance. We should therefore have a stronger sense of urgency.

Nor is there any reason for our view to adversely affect our personal holiness. Holiness is to be sought after by all who follow the Lord Jesus; and those who hold that He may return at any time and usher in the Last Judgment have as much or more to fear as those who believe in several different judgment days.

After the Olivet Discourse, the Lord gave the disciples two parables to show them how to live. I believe those parables are just as appropriate for modern disciples as they were for the original disciples. The first was the parable of the ten virgins (Matthew 25:1-13). Without arguing the details of the parable I believe it was clearly the Lord's intent for the disciples to understand one thing from this parable: they were to *be ready*, they were to be alert, for they did not know when He would return.

The equally important parable of the talents (Matthew 25:14-30) was to alert them to the fact that they were to use the time before his return wisely; they were to *be resourceful.* They were to invest their lives for God. These two parables speak to us of the importance of *salvation* and *sanctification.* To be ready, we must be saved. To be resourceful, we must exercise holiness, that is sanctification. It is not by mistake that our Lord immediately followed these two parables with a portrayal of the final judgment (Matthew 25:31-46). Those who are ready and resourceful will be given eternal life while those who have rejected Christ and holiness will be condemned to hell.

Chapter Seventeen

Where Do We Go from Here?

Those of us who have come to accept and understand a more reformed view of Christ's return must somehow tell others of our views. We must use mass media more effectively than we have in the past. This has been made more possible by Internet and Web sites that make information readily available. The "playing field" has become more level—outlets are available for views that are not popularly held to be discussed—but much remains to be done. DVDs can be produced at minimal expense in order to propagate the errors of dispensationalism. Books and booklets must be produced and promoted if we are to have any positive impact. If at all possible we must avoid offense, for there are many fine Christians who have been taught only the dispensational view. We are not just trying to make a point or have our voices heard, we are trying to present the truth of God plainly and clearly in order to help straighten out the perplexing thinking and teaching of those who have used media more effectively.

It seems to me that dispensationalism has affected the church in the same way that evolution has affected the world: it is commonly accepted without question. I also believe that those who study evolution and look for genuine understanding see just how ludicrous the whole concept is! My hope is that those who examine what the Bible really teaches about Christ's Second Coming will see through the fallacy of the dispensational system.

One Day

Just as America's founding fathers have liberated us with Constitutional freedoms, those who worked to give us the Bible in our own language have set us free as Christians. God has gifted the church with teachers, and we need to listen to them as we read the Bible on our own, seeking the aid of the Holy Spirit to help us understand.

Notes

[1] 1 Thessalonians 4:16; 1 Corinthians 15:52; Revelation 10:7

[2] Matthew 16:27, 28; 25:31; 1 Thessalonians 3:13; 4:14; 2 Thessalonians 1:7; Jude 14

[3] John 5:28, 29; 1 Corinthians 15:23; 2 Corinthians 5:10; 1 Thessalonians 4:16; Revelation 1:7

[4] Colossians 3:4; 1 Thessalonians 1:10; 5:9; Hebrews 9:28; 2 Peter 3:9, 10

[5] Romans 8:23; 1 Corinthians 15:50-52; 1 Thessalonians 4:15,16; Philippians 3:21; 1 John 3:2

[6] Matthew 16:27, 28; 25:31ff; 1 Corinthians 3:10-15; 2 Corinthians 5:10

[7] 2 Peter 3:7, 10, 11; Hebrews 10:27

[8] Matthew 25:41; Jude 6:7; Revelation 20:15

[9] 1 Corinthians 15:24

[10] 1 Corinthians 15:26; Revelation 20:14

[11] 2 Peter 3:12, 13; Revelation 21:1

[12] 1 Corinthians 15:24

[13] 1 Corinthians 15:28

[14] Revelation 10:7

[15] 1 Corinthians 2:14-16

[16] Philip Mauro was a patent lawyer in the early 1900s who devoted much of his life to the study and teaching of the Scriptures. He prepared the arguments against evolution in the well-known "Monkey-Scopes" trials.

[17] Sproul, R.C. *Now, That's a Good Question!* Wheaton, IL: Tyndale House, 1996. 47. Print.

[18] 1 Peter 5:8

[19] The Anti-Christ is an evil person who will inflict terrible sufferings on those who belong to Christ. The image varies from expositor to expositor, but the concept remains somewhat the same.

[20] Bray, John L. *The Coming of Christ in First and Second Thessalonians*, 1981. 18. Print.

[21] Bromiley, Geoffrey W. *Theological Dictionary of the New Testament*, Grand Rapids, MI: Eerdmans/Paternoster, 1985. 625. Print.

[22] Woodrow, Ralph *Great Prophecies of the Bible*, 1989. Part Four: The Anti-Christ. Print.

[23] Ralph Woodrow's newsletter of March 1986 shows how people have contrived to make people such as Ellen White, Sun Moon, and Kissinger into the Anti-Christ. Systems such as computers and the European Economic Community and even companies like Proctor and Gamble have been accused! More recently we have seen books that present Gorbachev and Saddam Hussein as the Anti-Christ.

[24] Jesus came to bear witness to the truth (John 18:37); to bring division (Matthew 10:35; Luke 12:51,52); to fulfill prophecy (Matthew 5:17); to call sinners (Matthew 9:13; Mark 2:17; Luke 5:32); to die on our behalf (John 12:27); to do the will of God (John 6:38) to give us abundant life (John 10:10). Nowhere does Jesus say or intimate that He came to establish a kingdom on earth for the Jews.

[25] Larken, Clarence *The Greatest Book on "Dispensational Truth" in the World.* Chart #36: "The Prophetic Days of Scripture. Print.

[26] *A Translators Handbook to the Gospel of Luke*, New York, NY: United Bible Societies, 1971. 671. Print.

[27] *Encyclopedia Britannica.* Vol. 12. Encyclopedia Britannica, 1973. 1054. Print.

[28] *Encyclopedia Judaica.* Vol 3. *Encyclopedia Judaica.* 49-50. Print.

[29] Jesus regards those who have genuine faith in and love for God as the children of Abraham while those who were closer to Abraham by blood were often considered children of the Devil.

[30] Stowell, Joseph *Eternity*. Grand Rapids, MI: Discovery House, 2006. 171. Print.

Note to the Reader

As you read and reflect on this booklet please do not hesitate to send me your insights at *dbcollver@yahoo.com*. I value your thoughts and will consider them for future revisions.

Additional copies can be purchased from Amazon.com.

The night is far spent, the Day is at hand!

Live as if you thought Christ might come at any time. Do everything as if you did it for the last time. Say everything as if you said it for the last time. Read every chapter in the Bible as if you did not know whether you would be allowed to read it again. Pray every prayer as if you felt that it might be your last opportunity. Hear every sermon as if you were hearing once and for ever. This is the way to be found ready. This is the way to turn Christ's second coming to good account. This is the way to put on the armor of light.

John Charles Ryle
1816-1900

Printed in Great Britain
by Amazon.co.uk, Ltd.,
Marston Gate.